SISTER CITIES: SIDE BY SIDE

Keeping Informed / Informándose. Wilbert Thompson, affectionately known in Puerto Cabezas as "The Spirit," reads EL NUEVO DIARIO.

SISTER CITIES: SIDE BY SIDE

PHOTOGRAPHS OF
PUERTO CABEZAS, NICARAGUA AND BURLINGTON, VERMONT
BY DAN HIGGINS

with a foreword by Alexander Cockburn

Green Valley Film and Art, Inc.
Burlington, Vermont
1988

Dedication

This book is dedicated to the more than 10,000 civilians and combatants who lost their lives in the Contra war.

It is our wish to share with other communities the riches and benefits that we in Burlington have gained by coming to know the people of Nicaragua, in particular those of the Atlantic Coast. We believe that, if "people to people" programs were embraced by more communities across the United States, the making of war on other countries would become more difficult — perhaps, one day, impossible.

Library of Congress Catalog Number: 88-081543

ISBN: 0-9614313-1-8 (softcover)

Copyright 1988 ©Green Valley Film and Art, Inc.

Publisher:
Green Valley Film and Art, Inc.
209 College Street, Burlington, Vermont 05401
(802) 658-2523

First Edition, June, 1988

Printed in Vermont, USA

Edited by Barry Snyder
Produced by Doreen Kraft
Designed by Leslie Fry

TABLE OF CONTENTS

ACKNOWLEDGEMENTS

We wish to thank all of the many individuals, organizations, and businesses whose contributions made this book possible. Our special thanks to the following for their exceptional generosity:

Christopher Lloyd
Plumsock Fund
Queen City Printers Inc.
William and Mary Lloyd
Champlain Color Corporation
Georgia Lloyd
David and Cybil Millstone

FOREWORD

Looking at these photographs for the first time on the walls of a bar in Burlington, I asked myself, "Could this kind of project have been done twenty years ago, where the images would not have been of Vermonters and Nicaraguans, but Vermonters and Vietnamese?" The answer I gave myself was, "No."

Like a lot of other people all those years ago I thought a great deal about the people of Vietnam, usually in images of suffering: prisoners in the tiger cages on Con Son island; villagers in the wake of a raid; victims. I thought of them above all in that dignified category, "the people of Vietnam." These days I think about "the people of Nicaragua," but I also think about *people in* Nicaragua, people I know or people I know about: Rene, who lost his legs to a land mine on the road to Wiliwi; the young men designing stamps in the Posts and Telegraph building; Xavier, on his new plot just south of Pantasma — all of them distinct figures in a political and social landscape. Vietnamese people mostly took the form of heroic concept or, to many young Americans, of targets seen through bombsights or gun barrels. A relative handful of Americans, opponents of the war, managed to visit North Vietnam or zones liberated by the NLF, but such trips were inevitably set to the formulaic rhythms of the solidarity tour, and the idiomatic specifics of the experience crushed by history's heavy agenda.

So there was a solidarity with a people, but not really a knowledge of, and sympathy with, persons. How different has been the experience with Nicaragua! Go almost anywhere in the United States and you will find people who have been in Nicaragua, to pick coffee or cotton, learn Spanish, be a Witness, help with a technical project, hitch-hike around, work on the Atlantic coast. There's a community of knowledge here, shared by many thousands of people for whom Nicaragua and the Nicaraguan revolution have been emotionally, intellectually, and linguistically (not forgetting financially) accessible in a way that Vietnam and its revolution never were. This was the community of knowledge and sympathy that was essential in keeping public opposition to Reagan's plans for Nicaragua at around 60 to 65 per cent, year after year.

There has been no stronger symbol of this community of interest than the Sister City movement. For one thing, in North America it has been an expression of civil resistance to the agenda of the state. Every time an inhabitant of Burlington, or one of the other sister cities and towns in the

United States, goes south in a delegation, every time a Nicaraguan delegation comes north, it's a thumb in the eye of the Reagan gang. And it's a truly textured solidarity, to which one can attach the word "popular" at its full range of meaning.

At the perceptual level, from the point of view of the first world confronting the third, what does that shop-worn word "imperialism" translate as? Most centrally, I think (having started experiencing the syndrome in England's oldest colony) blindness: the blindness of racism, the blindness of ignorance, which, of course, fuse into the blindness of fear.

This is where Dan Higgins' photographs come in. He writes in his introduction: "Showing the images and getting responses from the people in the pictures is an essential part of the photographic process for me . . . Context establishes meaning, and until one knows and trusts the photographer's motives, it is not unreasonable to be cautious about appearing before the camera." At first I thought those words were boilerplate, but after looking at his images and thinking about them, I came to see that they are not. The "objects" of his enquiry, in Burlington and Puerto Cabezas, became subjects, because they trusted him and (though this is in the realm of perhaps sentimental speculation) through his mediation look at and maybe begin to trust each other. Both groups look out into the world and challenge it, unlike Eugene Smith's Spanish villagers who looked inward because Smith set things up so that he appeared to be spying on them, for the edification of the readers of *Life* magazine.

Now this is no callow brothers-and-sisters-under-the-skin essay in the goofy idiom of *The Family of Man.* Here is the plenitude of the first world and the scarcity of the third: barber's shop and barber's porch; well-stocked bar and shebeen; pepper-steak sandwich on the menu board and a bowl of beans. These images make up the syntax of political and economic reality. The people with the bowl of beans aren't smiling and the people in the deli are. So as much as he proposes kinship Higgins records contrast; says here are the differences; asks how to deal with them; and answers: with Fraternity, that third great word in the slogan of the French revolution. In other words, with a generosity of spirit to which this book is testament.

Alexander Cockburn

INTRODUCTION

By the spring of 1986, the name Puerto Cabezas had become familiar to many of us in Burlington, Vermont. The community on Nicaragua's Atlantic coast had been made Burlington's sister city, and we received sporadic information from there during local efforts to raise material aid.

But my mental image of the town lacked substance, and I was frustrated that media images of Central America, rather than helping me imagine the place, actually distanced me from any real understanding of what life was like there. With their fixation on the spectacular, mainstream media ignore those ordinary, day-to-day social realities that provide the only trustworthy basis for understanding a society. By contrast, I have always learned the most about a community by photographing in those places where people regularly gather: the home, the school, the workplace, the social hall, the market.

I therefore began this project by asking a few very simple questions. If I were to find myself in Puerto Cabezas, where would I go for a cup of coffee, or a haircut, or to find a doctor? What would a classroom look like? A church? The fire department? My plan from the start was to ask the same questions of both Burlington and Puerto Cabezas and to produce a series of photographic pairs revealing equivalent categories of social life in these two communities. In June of 1986 I made the first pictures in Burlington, asked Vermonters what they would like to see of life in Puerto Cabezas, and left for Nicaragua.

July on Nicaragua's Atlantic coast is marked by continuous rain. The usually dusty, red clay streets of Puerto Cabezas become playponds for the frogs, whose ubiquitous croaking leaves no doubt as to the seriousness of the weather. Water pounds on corrugated metal roofs, and when people do move through the streets they run stooped under umbrellas or covered by flapping pieces of plastic. I found myself sequestered at the Restaurante Atlántico, eating homecooked meals, drinking Victoria Beers, and listening to old Jim Reeves recordings. I gave up any sense of urgency that I may have brought with me from Vermont and, like everyone else, waited for the rain to stop.

When it finally did, I made my first photographs of Puerto Cabezas. I had hoped to be able to print the images as I worked and display them as a way of involving the community, but technical conditions prevented me from doing that. Showing the images and getting responses from the people in the pictures is an essential part of the photographic process for

Dan Higgins photographing municipal employees, Burlington City Hall.

9

Sister Cities Photographs exhibited at Casa Popular de Cultura, Puerto Cabezas, August 1987.

me; in that interaction I often learn a great deal and am able to reassure the participants about my intentions. When, the following year, I was able to return with finished prints, I found my credibility enhanced, and was offered new opportunities to photograph additional groups.

Context establishes meaning, and until one knows and trusts the photographer's motives, it is not unreasonable to be cautious about appearing before the camera. One example of such suspicion occurred during my first week in Puerto Cabezas, when I photographed a group of barefoot shoeshine boys in the town park. Moments after I had made the picture (and fortunately stashed the film in my pocket), a young policeman invited me to accompany him to the neighboring police station. Although I had cleared my plans with government officials, the local police had not been informed and were uncertain about how to respond to a stranger photographing this eclectic group in the town square. Under the pretext that I may have photographed the police station, they invoked a law prohibiting the photographing of military installations and required me to hand over two rolls of exposed film from my camera bag.

Security concerns are indeed real in wartime Nicaragua, but I suspect that the police acted in part from their feeling that my choice of subject

Sister Cities Photographs
exhibited at Burlington City Hall,
January 1987.

matter was an attempt to reflect poorly on life there. Misgivings about fairness are not unjustified considering the castigation of revolutionary Nicaragua in the North American Press, where images often seem chosen to portray the wretchedness of living conditions there. Nicaraguans are sensitive not only about their image abroad but also at home, where the revolution has produced newly discovered feelings of national self-esteem. During my attempts to recover the film, I had the opportunity to talk with several officials who expressed concern that my exhibition of the comparison of life in Burlington and Puerto Cabezas could have the deleterious effect of making Nicaraguans feel ashamed and dissatisfied.

Yet misgivings were not limited to Puerto Cabezas. In Burlington, where there is no war going on, I encountered some comparable hesitancy about participating in the project. Representatives of institutions were often uncomfortable because of what they perceived to be political overtones, and I discovered that many corporate organizations protect their image by prohibiting the making of photographs outside the control of their own public relations departments. One large organization sent me through so many bureaucratic channels that I never did get an opportunity to photograph its employees. The schools required permission slips signed by parents before any student could appear in the photos. After a while, I learned to bypass formal channels altogether. Most individuals, I discovered, were enthusiastic about being included in the project.

The staging of the photographs in this collection was done in complete collaboration with the participants. I generally visited groups at least once before the actual session with the camera. I would arrive with other pictures, talk about the project, and encourage those in each group to decide when and where we would make the picture, who would constitute the group, and what props or symbols would be included. Because there are no pictures here of the hardships, shortages, or frustrations of living in a society that is torn by war, I was criticized by one older gentleman in Puerto Cabezas for giving too "rosy" a picture of life there. This is not to deny that immense hardships exist in Nicaragua. But in these pictures people are putting their best image forward; they are defining themselves in terms of who they would like to be.

In both communities the question of representation was often openly discussed. In the elementary school in Burlington, class members had a lively debate about which direction the camera should face, finally deciding on a backdrop that included a class project and American flag. The firemen in Puerto Cabezas vacillated on whether to wear their helmets or to hold them, some worrying that wearing them might look foolish when there obviously was no fire. The courthouse workers in Puerto Cabezas went out of their way to request a picture of themselves in front of the building where they worked, saying that the work they did was important but little recognized. The women who did laundry at the Puerto Cabezas hospital insisted on appearing next to a clothes drier that had been sent to them from Burlington.

Sometimes the choice of props was obvious, as, for example, the pie and coffee in the shot of the diner and beans and rolls in the shot of the comedería. At other times, leaving the decisions up to the participants produced unexpected results. The librarians in Puerto Cabezas chose to be photographed in front of a display honoring FSLN founder Carlos Fonseca that celebrates the Nicaraguan struggle against foreign domination. I never could have foreseen that one of them would wear the bright yellow, Burger King "We do it your way" T-shirt, a serendipitous reminder that life refuses to be bound by the categories in which we try to confine it.

Over the two years it took me to make these photographs I exhibited the pairs in both communities. In January, 1987, the photographs first appeared in the Burlington City Hall before traveling to outlying Vermont communities and schools. In August of that same year many were exhibited

Waterfront, Burlington.

Waterfront, Puerto Cabezas.

in Puerto Cabezas at the Casa Popular de Cultura, where they were seen by several hundred people over a ten day period.

In both places, the photographs that people showed the most enthusiasm for were those of the individuals with whom they interacted on a daily basis. For the residents of Puerto Cabezas, a place where photographic supplies are rare, the experience of seeing large images of their community was extraordinary. Viewers would go up and touch the pictures of friends, and before the exhibit was over, the surfaces of several had been rubbed smooth by probing fingers. A group of the shoeshine boys twice managed raids on the gallery, with great resourcefulness reappropriating the picture of themselves from the show.

Yet as much as people enjoyed seeing their own pictures, it was in their comparison of the two pairs that they revealed most about their respective world views. Hardly anyone seeing the exhibit missed the material imbalance between the two communities. For some in Puerto Cabezas this comparison became a criticism. More than one older woman approached and told me, "How embarrassed we are that our clothes are not as nice as the ones the people wear to church in Burlington." In turn, Vermonters often responded with, "How lucky we are," or, "How sad it is that those people are so poor."

Making nacatamales.

Such imbalances are real, but North American affluence is not due to good luck, nor Nicaraguan impoverishment to anything for which the Nicaraguans should feel embarrassment. There are historical, political, and economic explanations for the disparity of wealth between the two societies. As I worked on these photographs, it was chilling to remember that during the past eight years of the Reagan administration the United States government had spent an estimated 15 billion dollars to punish Nicaragua and make life as intolerable as possible for people living there.

In Puerto Cabezas, the effects of that policy showed up everywhere, from the young people I met who had lost arms and legs in the war, to the shortages of basic supplies to feed and clothe the many displaced persons. The influx of refugees had swelled the population of the town from 13,000 in 1981 to 22,000 in 1987. When I arrived in 1987, there had been no flour for bread for almost three months, and the ration of rice was down to two pounds-per-person for three weeks. The value of the cordoba had fallen from approximately 50 to the dollar in 1981 to 20,000 to the dollar in 1987. Replacements for anything from guitar strings to parts for vehicles and industrial machines were impossible to obtain because of the crippling United States trade embargo.

The Reagan administration's not-so-secret war to destroy the Nicaraguan Revolution has never received the support of the American people. Reagan's portrayal of revolutionary Nicaragua as a closed and totalitarian society is seen as a transparent attempt to manipulate public opinion in the United States. His Cold War rhetoric has been countered by the stories of the many North Americans who have had the opportunity to visit Nicaragua and personally experience life there.

Still, the image most North Americans hold of Central America is that of a very dangerous and unfathomable place. Mainstream media promote that belief with their emphasis on images of suffering and violence, a collective picture which fails to take note of the strong and diverse social underpinnings that support people there. Too often we become numbed by what appears to be the hopeless turmoil of the region. Unable to relate to others as human beings like ourselves, we learn to think in terms of an innate difference between US and THEM.

My friend Jed Davis, who runs the Port Authority in Puerto Cabezas, has an ambitious plan for cutting through these misconceptions:

> "I would suggest that the Americans of every state in the United States — there are fifty states, right? — I would suggest that they start swapping people with Nicaragua. You take a plane load of Americans and send them down to one of the little towns in Central America and you load these planes up with people that can speak the language in the United States. Let them live for a week or two and send them back home. Simple.
>
> We aren't talking about governments. What we are talking about is people."

My hope in presenting these photographs is that they can help us in the United States recognize our authentic connections with the people of Central America. I like to think of this book as a small version of one of Jed's airplanes.

Dan Higgins

A PORTRAIT OF THE TWO SISTER CITIES

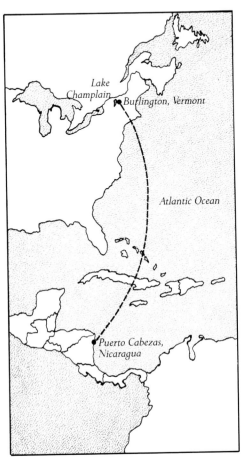

	Burlington	**Puerto Cabezas**
Location	Urban center on Lake Champlain	Port city on the Caribbean
Population	38,000	22,000
Anglo/white	98.5%	less than 1%
Indian	.2%	70%
Hispanic	.9%	20%
Black	.4%	10%
Climate	Temperate	Rainforest/tropical
Temperature	15°F January 70°F July	70°F
Rainfall	33″ yearly	200″ yearly
Major Languages	English, French	Miskito, Spanish, English
Major Religions	Catholic, Jewish, Protestant	Protestant (Moravian), Catholic, Indian spiritual practice
Economy	Hi-tech industry, machinery, maple, apple and dairy products, printing, tourism, medicine, education	Fishing, lumbering, subsistence agriculture, crafts

COMMENTARY

Dan Higgins is probably best known around Vermont for his photographs of the tiny mill town where he makes his home. As the neighbor of Vermont's largest city, Winooski has undergone the quintessential post-60's evolution from self-sustaining community to suburb, a change perfectly symbolized by the transformation of the old mills themselves into chic conglomerations of upscale offices, shops, restaurants, and apartments. Higgins' decade-long task has been to seek out and record the vestiges of the older community's identity among the people and in the places where it is maintained. The role he has defined for himself is an uncommon one in today's commercial art world: the role of social preservationist.

The Sister Cities Photographs are a direct descendant of Higgins' Winooski studies, and do not change the focus of his interests so much as geographically expand them. From the beleaguered ma-and-pa stores of the U.S. to the barren comederías of Nicaragua – in the totality of Higgins' work, they seem like not distant phenomena at all. Taken as a whole, these photographs help us to realize that the forces of social disintegration at work in the U.S. are not unrelated to those at work elsewhere in the world. And what better way might we come to understand the turmoil of places like Central America than in terms of a kind of international gentrification?

If political art is art which makes such connections explicit, the Sister Cities Photographs are a definitive example. A comparison of geographically and culturally disparate communities is the overt subject of the work, which has as its basic unit not the single image but the photographic pair. Burlington and Puerto Cabezas are sister cities, after all, only by formal declaration. The goal of these photographs is to help us understand the factual basis for a claim of kinship.

That is a goal toward which the medium of photography is ideally suited. The photograph has an unsurpassed capacity to record detail, and that record is, on some level, objective. Still, Higgins recognizes that the factual information contained in a photograph does not alone determine its meaning. Meaning is a matter that tends to lie in the context of the prevailing ideas in which a photograph is received. Thus, a photograph of a limbless Nicaraguan orphan contains a number of irreducible facts. But how we receive those facts, whether they enlighten us or get in the way of understanding, motivate us to action or fill us with a sense of hopelessness, is determined by our pre-existing categories of thought.

One of the ways Higgins has overcome these limitations is by liberating the photograph from the tyranny of the photographic instant. In the Sister Cities Photographs, the decisive moment of each photograph is actively planned for rather than left to chance, and arrived at in full collaboration with the photograph's participants. The essence of each photograph is theatrical rather than photojournalistic, the product of a process of distillation in which the photographer himself is dissolved. The images have the refreshing unpretentiousness of the official-group-shot photograph enshrined in yearbooks and annual reports, reminding one that what is important, for a change, is the subject and not the photographer's stance.

The other means by which the Sister Cities Photographs ascertain meaning is through the process of pairing itself. A single photograph is open to a multitude of interpretations; pairing it with another radically narrows the possibilities. In effect, the photographic pair creates a context for understanding which the isolated image does not possess. If, as Susan Sontag maintains, photography has worked to deny the interconnectedness and continuity of the world, these photographs work in the opposite direction, toward putting the world back together, two pieces at a time.

The result, in any case, is a remarkable iconographic record that cuts through the thick camouflage of abstractions justifying our aggression against Nicaragua and radically redefines the terms of the current political debate. With startling simplicity and directness, the Sister Cities Photographs compel us to recognize both the commonality of human needs and responses in different countries and the imbalance of resources available to meet them. The first recognition militates against the carefully nurtured myth that war, any war, can exist without human loss. The second militates against the further myth that such wars are beyond our control or understanding.

The Sister Cities Photographs are not photographs which belong, in the usual sense, to the photographer. They belong to the people and the communities comprising them. The brazenness of the photojournalist and the presumption of art photographer are here replaced by another quality, by a sense of respect and cooperation. What these photographs contain is a sense of obligation and commitment to something beyond themselves – that is, a moral sense. It's a quality as rare in the sphere of art as it is in politics.

Barry Snyder

THE PHOTOGRAPHS

Municipal workers, Burlington City Hall.

Trabajadores municipales, Junta Municipal de Reconstruction.

Barbería.

23

College Stylists Barbershop.

Oasis Diner.

Comedería contigo Loteria Popular.

Lavanderas , Grey Memorial Hospital.

Linen workers, Medical Center Hospital of Vermont.

Sneaker's Jazz Ensemble.

Cooperativa de los Artistas.

Downtown Quick Stop and Deli.

Una tienda, calle principal.

Escuela Publica.

Edmunds Elementary School.

Taxi de Puerto Cabezas.

B and B Taxi.

Chittenden County Courthouse.

Tribunal de la Region.

Congregación, Iglesia Central de los Moravos.

Congregation, First Unitarian Universalist Church.

Skateboarders, City Hall Park.

40

Lustradores, Plaza Central.

Hot Dog Lady.

43   *Vendedora de comida.*

Cuerpo de Bomberos.

Central Fire Station, Burlington.

Juventud Sandinista, Casa Julio Downs.

46

Girl Scout Troop 217.

Biblioteca José Ferer.

Fletcher Free Library.

Centro de Salud.

Community Health Center.

Volunteers, Vermont Army National Guard.

Reservista militar con su familia.

Lavandería, Barrio Nuevo.

Gaslight Laundromat.

Lecciones de musica, a la casa de Sr. Clifford Cole.

Cooking classes, North End Community Center.

Lake Champlain Transportation workers.

Estibadores.

Daily Planet.

Restaurante de Shyrla.

Lady of St. Anne Society, St. Joseph's Church.

Hijos and Hijas del Rey, Iglesia de los Moravos.

HIGHLIGHTS OF THE PUERTO CABEZAS/BURLINGTON SISTER CITY PROGRAM

September 1984. The Board of Aldermen vote unanimously to establish a sister city relationship between Burlington, Vermont and Puerto Cabezas, Nicaragua.

March 1985. First delegation from Burlington visits Puerto Cabezas, officially proclaiming the beginning of this new international relationship. Mayor Bernard Sanders visits during 5th anniversary of the Nicaraguan Revolution.

Winter 1985. Public meetings and educational forums begin to involve local people in the program and inform them about Puerto Cabezas.

Summer 1985. Burlington begins an emergency material aid drive to send medical supplies and equipment, educational materials, food, and clothing to the beleaguered Atlantic coast of Nicaragua.

Fall 1985. Visitors come from Puerto Cabezas and bring the reality of the war home to Burlington. Among them are the governor of the region that includes our sister city, a Miskito lawyer who is a member of the National Autonomy Commission, and a poet.

January 1986. Pete Seeger gives a benefit concert to help the Sister City Program.

April 1986. Ship sets sail for Puerto Cabezas carrying the largest shipment of material aid ever to reach the Atlantic coast. Burlington, the organizer of this historic voyage, contributes 40 tons of goods, and 500 tons are donated by other aid organizations around the U.S.

June 1986. Documentary by local filmmakers about Puerto Cabezas, the war, and the importance of sister city programs is completed and travels around Vermont.

July 1986. Delegation from Burlington joins North American Indian delegation to take part in the International Symposium on Autonomy (indigenous rights) held in Managua.

November 1987. Sister City initiated ballot referendum condemning Contra aid is approved by Burlington voters in November election.

January 1987. Burlington is material aid organizer for National Peace Ship Coalition, pulling together 18 organizations from three countries to send a total of 240 tons of emergency aid to Nicaragua.

February 1987. Brigade of carpenters and plumbers travel to Puerto Cabezas to help build a playground for the young people and fix the hospital building.

Summer/Fall 1987. Burlington helps other Vermont towns set up Sister City Programs and "twin" organizations from Vermont with similar ones in Puerto Cabezas. (For example, school to school and library to library.)

October 1987. Carpenters brigade helps King Street Youth Program with construction project at their center in Burlington.

January 1988. Beginning of yearly material aid drive.

March 1988. Area gardeners join together and start a family gardens project for Puerto Cabezas.

April 1988. With grant from local food cooperative Burlington plans to set up farming cooperative in Puerto Cabezas.